The Wonderfully Weird Kids™

A Letter to Sensitives Everywhere

Visit us online, anytime:

www.WeirdKids.Club

This book is dedicated to

ALL Sensitives

everywhere!

A Weird Kid sees what
no one else sees.

A Weird Kid talks to the
dogs and the trees.

A Weird Kid knows when
someone was bad.

A Weird Kid can feel
when someone is sad.

A Weird Kid may hurt
and not know why.

Maybe a sad soul
has just passed them by.

A Weird Kid feels that they don't quite fit.
So in a corner they quietly sit.

A Weird Kid's not happy when music is loud.
A Weird Kid hates being in a big crowd.

A Weird Kid might hide as the world goes by.
A Weird Kid may be "sensitive" or shy.

Weird Kids are smart geeks and nerds.
We stay far away from the thundering herds.

We process things deeply, so quick and so much.
We feel every feeling, all in a bunch.

While you may feel like you're a bit weird,
I'm here to tell you, my sweet little dear...

YOU carry a great

and natural power...

every year,

every month,

every day,

every hour.

You have a purpose,
a path, and a light

that is very well hidden,
far out of sight.

You're greatly needed - to help and to heal.
YOU have the ability with all that you feel.

YOU remember the lessons learned from the past.
Some call you truly, you're an EMPATH!

Strangers don't know
you have this great power.

They may TRY to push you
and make you cower.

Breathe...
4 counts in -
and 4 counts out.

Just try it and feel
what it's all about.

Make a close friend,

with whom you can share

your abilities and fears...

Someone who cares.

For there's power in numbers
This much is true.

With support and comfort, you
can be your TRUE YOU.

So play with your gift,
whatever it be.

Practice, experiment,
stand confidently.

You are the change for which most of us strive.
YOU have what we search for all of our lives.

You are wonderful, this much is true.
Stay being you... Be true to YOU.

Help heal this world,
as you are meant to...

Help those around you.
Be YOU through and through!

We're changing the world,
one kid at a time...

Letting everyone know
it's OK to shine!!

I Wonder Ideas...

Stuff To Talk About

- ## Are <u>YOU</u> a Wonderfully Weird Kid?

- ## <u>HOW</u> so?

  Some kids have 'sensitive' sight or hearing. Some kids have 'healing hands' - and some feel everything extra deeply. There are so many ways to be Wonderfully Weird. What are <u>your</u> ways?

- ## How does it <u>FEEL</u> to you to be a Wonderfully Weird Kid?

  Scared? Strong? Excited?

More Weird Kids books are on the way:

A Letter to Weird Parents

The World the Weird Kids Created

The Weird Kids Clubhouse

A Weird Kid Opens Their Gift

A Weird Kid Shares Their Gift

A Weird Kid Faces the Dark

A Weird Kid Meets Their Guides

www.WeirdKids.Club

- Join our email list - You'll be the first to know when new Weird Kids books come out
- Bulk Discounts, Bonus Content, and "Sensitivity Central" for Weird Kids (& Families)

Author
Dr. Rev Laura Palmer

Dr. Rev Laura Palmer is a Highly Sensitive Person Cheerleader. When she's not working with Sensitives, she can be found playing with fairies and dragons.

EXCITO.PRESS

Illustrator
Adrianne Smith

Adrianne Smith is a Reiki Master for humans & other animals, and Mom of five Wonderfully Weird Kids. When she's not wrangling kids, she's out wrangling horses.